SCHOLASTIC
News
Nonfiction Readers®

We Are Alike, We Are Different

By Janice Behrens

Children's Press®
An Imprint of Scholastic Inc.
New York Toronto London Auckland Sydney
Mexico City New Delhi Hong Kong
Danbury, Connecticut

These content vocabulary word builders are for grades 1–2.

Subject Consultant: Eli J. Lesser, MA, Director of Education, National Constitution Center, Philadelphia, Pennsylvania

Reading Consultant: Cecilia Minden-Cupp, PhD, Early Literacy Consultant and Author, Chapel Hill, North Carolina

Photographs ©2010: Alamy Images: 13 bottom left (BananaStock0107), 15 bottom left (Rolf Bruderer/Blend Images), 13 bottom right (Tom Grill), 11 center right (Martin Harvey), 12, 22 top right (D. Hurst), 14 (JupiterImages/Comstock Images), 4, 22 bottom (JupiterImages/Polka Dot), 15 center right (John Lund/Tiffany Schoepp/Blend Images), 7 bottom left (Celia Mannings), 13 top left (Picture Partners), 13 top right (Larry Williams/LWA/Blend Images); Fotolia/Tjui Tjioe: 7 top right; Getty Images: 7 bottom right (Scott T. Baxter), 11 top right (Jonathan Kirn), 15 bottom right (Pat LaCroix), 11 bottom left (Daniel Pangbourne), 7 top left (Kris Timken), 15 top right (Yellow Dog Productions); iStockphoto: 10 (Charles Benavidez), 1, 9 (Jani Bryson), 16, 23 bottom (Olena Druzhynina), 17 top left (Rich Legg), 6 center, 22 top center (Jason Lugo), 6 bottom right (George Pchemyan), 5 (Daniela Andreea Spyropoulos), 6 top right (Artur Tomasz Komorowski); PhotoEdit/Richard Hutchings: back cover, 17 bottom, 17 top right; ShutterStock, Inc./Roman Sigaev: 6 left, 22 top left; Superstock, Inc./Ingram Publishing: 15 center left; VEER: cover, 11 top left, 20, 21 (Blend Images Photography), 23 center (Comstock Photography), 8, 23 top (Corbis Photography), 11 bottom right (Image Source Photography), 2, 15 top left (Juice Images Photography), 19 (Stockbyte Photography).

Art Direction and Production: Scholastic Classroom Magazines

Library of Congress Cataloging-in-Publication Data

Behrens, Janice, 1972-
We are alike, we are different / Janice Behrens.
    p. cm. – (Scholastic news nonfiction readers)
Includes bibliographical references and index.
ISBN 13: 978-0-531-21347-6 (lib. bdg.) 978-0-531-21447-3 (pbk.)
ISBN 10: 0-531-21347-1 (lib. bdg.) 0-531-21447-8 (pbk.)
1. Multiculturalism–Juvenile literature. 2. Cultural pluralism–Juvenile literature.
3. Interpersonal relations–Juvenile literature. I. Title. II. Series.
HM1271.B44 2009   305.8–dc22 2009007316

1 2 3 4 5 6 7 8 9 10 R 18 17 16 15 14 13 12 11 10 09

CONTENTS

We Are All People

We are all alike. We are all **people**.

We are all different, too. We do not look the same.

people

How We Look

We are all alike. We all wear **clothes**.

We wear different things. One girl may wear a scarf on her head. Another may wear a cowboy hat.

What do you like to wear?

clothes

What do you wear on your head?

7

We are all alike. We all have **skin**.

Some people have lighter skin. Some people have darker skin.

Every skin color is a beautiful color.

skin

We are alike. We have **hair**.

You can have long hair or short hair. You can have straight hair or curly hair. You can have braids or spiked hair.

Hooray for hair! How do you like to wear your hair?

hair

11

Food and Fun

We are all alike. We all eat food. We like to eat different things.

Some of us eat noodles with **chopsticks**. Many of us like burgers. Some of us love pickles!

What do you love to eat?

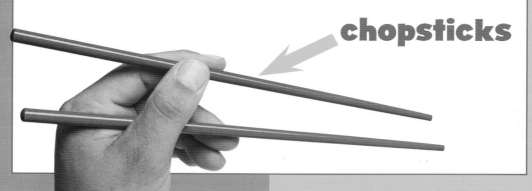

chopsticks

We are all alike. We all like to have fun.

People have fun in different ways. Some play ball. Some play jump rope. Some play the **tuba**!

What do you like to play?

tuba

15

Getting Around

We are all alike. We all need to get around. We move in different ways.

Some of us walk on our own. Some of us need help to move around. We might use a **wheelchair**.

wheelchair

We are all different.

We have different skin.
We have different hair. We
eat different foods. We
move differently.

We are all alike, too. We
can all be friends!

WE ALL SAY HELLO!

We are all alike. We all use language. We speak many different languages.

> **We say Bonjour! in French.**

> **We say Marhaba! in Arabic.**

> **We say Hello! in English.**

What language do you speak? How do you say hello?

e say
i hao! in
hinese.

We say
Jambo! in
Swahili.

We say
Hola! in
Spanish.

YOUR NEW WORDS

chopsticks (**chop**-stiks) thin sticks used to pick up and eat food

clothes (klohz) things that people wear, such as pants, shirts, or dresses

hair (hair) the thin, flexible strands that grow on people's heads and bodies

people (**pee**-puhl) human beings

in (skin) the outer layer on the
bodies of people and animals

tuba (**too**-buh) a large brass
musical instrument that makes
a deep sound

heelchair (**weel**-chair) a chair with wheels,
for people who need
help to move around

INDEX

FIND OUT MORE

Book:

Wells, Rosemary. *Yoko*. New York: Hyperion, 1998.

Website:

PBS Kids
http://pbskids.org/arthur/games/connectworld/index.html

MEET THE AUTHOR

Janice Behrens is a writer and Scholastic editor. She lives in Brooklyn, New York, with her family.